W9-CZJ-748

A Time
for Friends

A Time for Friends

Bernard J. Weiss
Senior Author
Reading and Linguistics

Eldonna L. Evertts
Language Arts

Susan B. Cruikshank
Reading and Language Arts

Loreli Olson Steuer
Reading and Linguistics

Lyman C. Hunt
General Editor—Satellite Books

Holt
Basic
Reading

Level 8

HOLT, RINEHART AND WINSTON, PUBLISHERS
New York ● Toronto ● Mexico City ● London ● Sydney ● Tokyo

ISBN 0-03-061389-2
5 071 987654

Acknowledgments:

Grateful acknowledgment is made to the following authors and publishers:

Child Life and Elizabeth Upham McWebb for "At Mrs. Appleby's." Copyright 1944 by Elizabeth Upham McWebb. Used by permission.

Thomas Y. Crowell Company for "New Neighbors" from *In One Door and Out the Other* by Aileen Fisher. Copyright © 1969 by Aileen Fisher. Used by permission.

William Cole, as agent for Shel Silverstein, for "Mr. Spats." Copyright © 1966 by Shel Silverstein. Used by permission.

020.The Dial Press for "All the Lassies," adapted from *All the Lassies* by Liesel Moak Skorpen. Copyright © 1970 by Liesel Moak Skorpen. Used by permission.

Doubleday & Company, Inc., and John Farquharson, Ltd., for "The Little Red Flower," adapted from *The Little Red Flower* by Paul Tripp. Copyright © 1968 by Paul Tripp. Used by permission.

E. P. Dutton & Co., Inc., for "The Camel Who Went for a Walk," adapted from *The Camel Who Took a Walk* by Jack Tworkov. Copyright 1951 by Jack Tworkov. Used by permission.

Harper & Row, Publishers, Inc., for "André" from *Bronzeville Boys and Girls* by Gwendolyn Brooks. Copyright © 1956 by Gwendolyn Brooks Blakely. Used by permission.

Hastings House, Publishers, Inc., for "Where Have You Been?" from *Where Have You Been?* by Margaret Wise Brown. Copyright 1952 by Margaret Wise Brown. Used by permission.

Holt, Rinehart and Winston, Publishers for "Just About," from *Just Around the Corner* by Leland B. Jacobs. Copyright © 1964 by Leland B. Jacobs. Used by permission.

J. B. Lippincott Company for "How to Tell the Top of a Hill," from *The Reason for the Pelican* by John Ciardi. Copyright © 1969 by John Ciardi. Used by permission.

Macmillan Publishing Co., Inc., for "The Swings in the Park" by Cathy McGlynn. Compiled by Charles E. Schaefer and Kathleen C. Mellor. Copyright © 1971 by Center for Urban Education. Used by permission.

Random House, Inc., for "Camel," from *The Wild and Wooly Animal Book* by Nita Jonas. Copyright © 1961 by Nita Jonas. Used by permission.

Henry Regnery Co., for "Maggie in the Middle," adapted from *The One in the Middle Is the Green Kangaroo* by Judy Blume. Copyright © 1969 by Judy Blume. Used by permission.

Scholastic Magazines, Inc., for "That's What Friends Are For," adapted from *That's What Friends Are For* by Florence Parry Heide and Sylvia Worth Van Clief. Copyright © 1968 by Florence Parry Heide and Sylvia Worth Van Clief. Used by permission.

Franklin Watts, Inc., for "The New Spring Hats," adapted from *Belinda's New Spring Hat* by Eleanor Clymer. Copyright © 1969 by Eleanor Clymer. Used by permission.

Art Credits:

Marie Michal, pages 14 − 27
Ethel Gold, pages 28 − 45, 188 − 199
Patty Churchill, pages 46 − 47
Sven Lindman, pages 46, 122, 186 (career graphics)
Lester Abrams, pages 48 − 62
Phil Smith, pages 64 − 83
Ellen Olean, page 84
Viewpoint Graphics, Inc., page 85
Tom Leigh, pages 88 − 105
Marvin Mattelson, page 106
Tim and Greg Hildebrandt, page 107

Table of Contents

UNIT ONE

ALL KINDS OF FRIENDS

The Swings in the Park
a poem by Cathy McGlynn   12

Kim and Rosa *a story*
   The Apartment House   15
   The Elevator   20

Two Friends *a story by Annie Moorecroft*
   Edward and Peter   29
   The New Boy   35
   Three Friends   41

♥CAREERS: Friends of the Neighborhood 46

6

That's What Friends Are For *a story by*
Florence Parry Heide and Sylvia Worth Van Clief   48

To Give Advice Is Very Nice
a poem by Florence Parry Heide and
Sylvia Worth Van Clief   62

LANGUAGE: **What Did You Say?**   63

The Little Red Flower *a story by Paul Tripp*
   A Green Thumb   64
   Who Can Save the Flower?   70
   New Flowers   77

At Mrs. Appleby's
a poem by Elizabeth Upham McWebb   84

LANGUAGE: Two Into One   85

UNIT TWO
ALL KINDS OF FAMILIES

André *a poem by Gwendolyn Brooks*   86

Maggie in the Middle *a story by Judy Blume*
  The Middle Is No Place To Be   88
  Maggie Gets a Part   93
  The One in the Middle Is the Green Kangaroo   99

Just About *a poem by Leland B. Jacobs*   106

LANGUAGE: Short Cut   107

The New Spring Hats *a story by Eleanor Clymer*
  Hats Everywhere   108
  Belinda's Hat   115

Mr. Spats *a poem by Shel Silverstein*   121

CAREERS: Friends of the Family   122

All the Lassies *a story by Liesel Moak Skorpen*
   Just One Wish   124
   All the Lassies and Walter   129

Bert's Berries *a story by George McCue*
   Bert   134
   A Happy Bear   138

LOOKING AT ART: The Family in Art   145

A Quiet Walk *a poem by Pete Shiflet*   153

LANGUAGE: One or More?   154

LANGUAGE: Three Guesses   155

9

UNIT THREE
ALL KINDS OF
PLACES TO GO

How to Tell the Top of a Hill
a poem by John Ciardi   156

A Place for Carmen *a story*   158

New Neighbors *a poem by Aileen Fisher*   170

The Browns Say Good-by *a story*
   Moving Day   171
   The New House   178

   ๑ CAREERS: People on the Go   186

Our Trip *a story by Annie Moorecroft*
  Two Washingtons   188
  Washington, D.C.   194

LANGUAGE: Slow Down!   201

The Camel Who Went for a Walk
  a story by Jack Tworkov   202

Camel *a poem by Nita Jonas*   215

Where Have You Been?
  a poem by Margaret Wise Brown   217

NEW WORDS   230

ALL KINDS OF FRIENDS

The swings in the park
They are so lonely looking
Until you play there

—Cathy McGlynn, Age 9

Kim
and
Rosa

14

PART ONE
The Apartment House

Kim lived in a big apartment house.
She lived in apartment 17B
with her mother and daddy
and sister and brother.
Kim had lots of friends
in the apartment house.

One of Kim's friends was Rosa.
She lived in apartment 6B.
When Kim wanted to go to see Rosa,
her big sister had to take her.
When it was time to go home,
Kim's sister had to come to get her.

Kim didn't like to have
her sister take her places.
She wanted to go alone.
But her mother said, "You're
too *little!*"

One day Kim's sister was not at home
when Kim wanted to go to see Rosa.

"Will you take me to Rosa's apartment,
Mother?" asked Kim.

Mother said, "I don't have time
to take you, Kim.

But you are a big girl now.

You can go alone."

That was all Kim's mother had to say.
Kim ran out of her apartment.

She was going to Rosa's apartment alone!

The girls played at Rosa's apartment all morning.
Then Rosa's brother came home
with some friends.

"Boys make too much noise," said Kim.
"Do you want to go up to my apartment?
It's quiet there."

"Yes," said Rosa.
"Let me tell Mother where I'm going."

PART TWO
The Elevator

Kim and Rosa got into the elevator.
They looked at all the buttons.
They tried to reach the one that said (17.)
But they couldn't reach it.

"What are we going to do?"
asked Rosa.

"Maybe if I jump, I can reach 17,"
said Kim.

Kim jumped up.
She did reach a button, but not 17.

The elevator went up to

11, 12, 13....

Then it stopped, and the door opened.

"This is not my floor," said Kim.

"Let me jump up," said Rosa.
"Maybe I can reach 17."

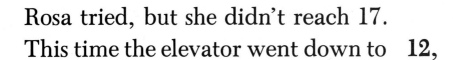

Rosa tried, but she didn't reach 17.
This time the elevator went down to   12,

11,

10.

Then it stopped.
And the door opened.

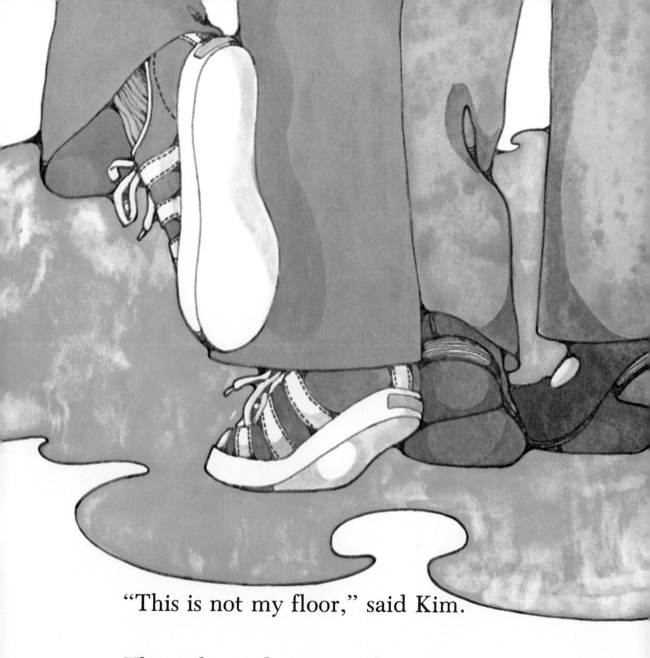

"This is not my floor," said Kim.

The girls tried again and again.
The elevator went up and down.
But it did not go to Kim's floor.
Kim tried to reach the button again.
This time the elevator went down to **6.**

"This is my floor," said Rosa.

Rosa got out of the elevator.
"I'll be back," she said to Kim.

"What are you going to do?"
asked Kim.
"Are you going to get someone?"

"No," said Rosa.
"We can go up to 17 alone.
You will see."

Rosa ran back into her apartment.
She came back with a big book.

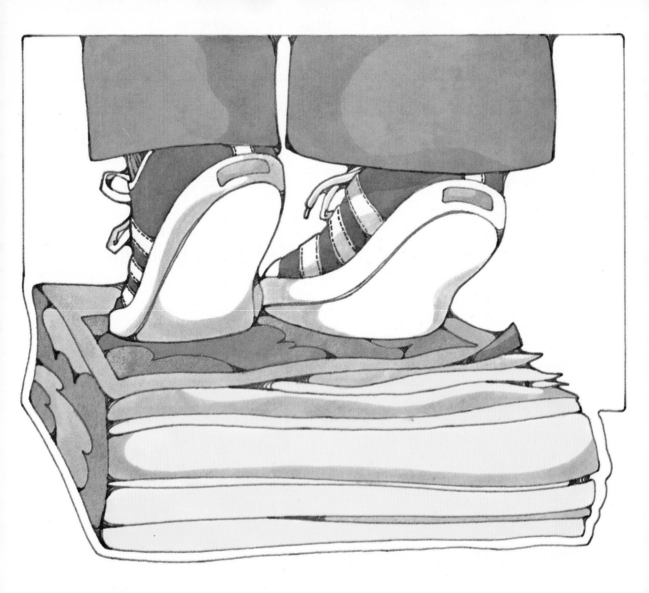

Rosa and Kim got into the elevator.
Rosa put the book on the floor
by the buttons.
Kim got up on the book.
This time she did reach 17.
The elevator went up to

7, 8, 9, 10, 11, 12.

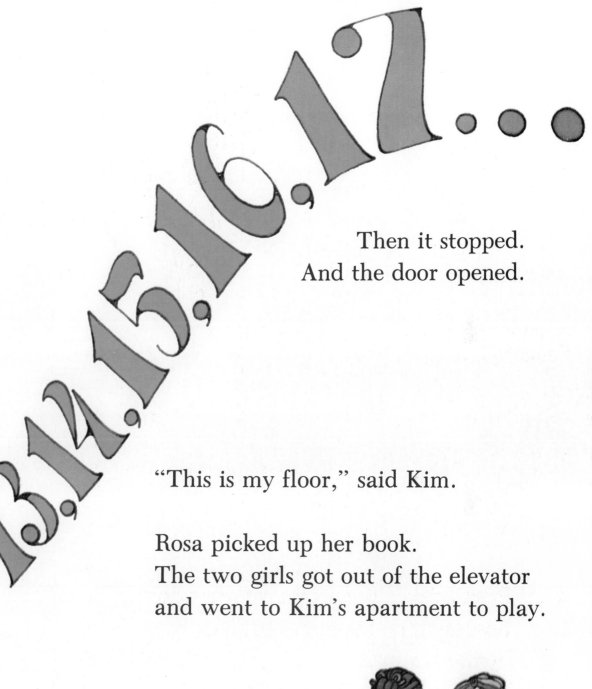

13,14,15,16,17...

Then it stopped.
And the door opened.

"This is my floor," said Kim.

Rosa picked up her book.
The two girls got out of the elevator
and went to Kim's apartment to play.

Annie Moorecroft

Two Friends

PART ONE
Edward and Peter

Edward and Peter were old friends.
When they were little,
they played all day.
One day they would play
at Edward's house.
The next day they would play
at Peter's house.
Some nights Edward would sleep
at Peter's house.
Some nights Peter would sleep
at Edward's house.

When they got big,
the boys went to school.
At school they played and worked
like old friends.
Peter would read to Edward.
Edward would read to Peter.

Sometimes after school Peter would go
to Edward's house.
They would have cookies.
Sometimes they would go to Peter's house.
They would have apples at Peter's house.
People said that Peter and Edward were
like brothers.

One morning Edward went
to Peter's house.
Peter's mother came to the door.

"Peter is sick," she said.
"He won't be going to school."

"That's too bad," said Edward.

Edward went to school alone.
He played with some friends.
Then he read books with them.
But it was a bad day for Edward.
He was lonely.
He wanted to be with Peter.

After school Edward went home.
He had no one to play with
but his dog.

"Do you get lonely when I'm at school?"
he asked his dog.

"He gets lonely in the afternoon,"
said Edward's mother.
"That's when he looks for you.
He wants you to come home."

"I'll play with you," said Edward.
"You won't have to be lonely."

Edward played with his dog all afternoon.
But it was a lonely day.
"It's too bad Peter's sick," he thought.

The next morning Edward went
to Peter's house.
Peter came to the door.

"I'm all right this morning,"
he said.
"I'm going to school."

"That's good," said Edward.
"I was lonely when you were sick."

"We can play at my house
after school," said Peter.

"No," said Edward.
"We have to go to my house.
Then we can play with my dog.
He gets lonely, too."

PART TWO

The New Boy

One day Edward went to Peter's house.
Edward did not go alone.

"This is my new friend, Jimmy,"
he said to Peter.
"He lives in the new house next door.
Jimmy has a cat."

The boys went to school.
Jimmy told Edward about his cat.
Edward told Jimmy about his dog.

Edward said, "Peter has a frog."

Peter told Jimmy about his frog.

"Don't let my cat see your frog,"
said Jimmy.
"Cats don't like frogs."

Peter didn't like it
when Jimmy said that.

At school Edward and Jimmy looked
at pictures.
Edward asked Peter to look
at the pictures, too.

"No," said Peter.
"I don't like Jimmy.
I don't want to play with him.
If you like Jimmy,
then you can't be my friend."

"If I can't be your friend,
then you can't be my friend,"
said Edward.

That morning Peter didn't read
to Edward.
And Edward didn't read to Peter.
After school Peter didn't go
to Edward's house.
He went home alone.

"Where is Edward?" Peter's mother asked.

"Edward has a new friend,"
said Peter.
"He isn't going to come here to play.
He's at Jimmy's house."

"Who is Jimmy?" asked Peter's mother.

"He's a new boy," said Peter.
"And he's Edward's new friend."

"Can't Jimmy be your friend, too?
Can't all three of you play?"
asked Peter's mother.

"No," said Peter.
"I don't like Jimmy.
He isn't my friend.
And Edward isn't my friend.
And I don't want to play with them!"

PART THREE
Three Friends

The next day Peter had to walk
to school alone.
Edward walked with Jimmy.

At school Peter read books
and looked at pictures.
But it was no fun without Edward.
And he couldn't forget about Jimmy.

41

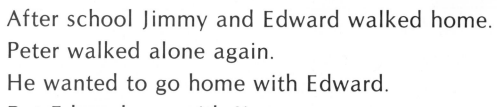

After school Jimmy and Edward walked home.
Peter walked alone again.
He wanted to go home with Edward.
But Edward was with Jimmy.
And Peter couldn't forget what Jimmy had said.

Jimmy and Edward stopped
at Jimmy's house.
Peter walked on by.
But Edward saw him.

"Peter, where are you going?"
asked Edward.

"Home," said Peter.

"Would you like to see Jimmy's cat?"
asked Edward.
"He's in the house."

"Yes," said Jimmy to Peter.
"He's a big cat.
Come in and see him."

"All right," said Peter.
"I'll take a look at your cat.
Then I have to go home."

Peter liked Jimmy's cat.
He forgot about not liking Jimmy.
He forgot about going home.
The three boys had lots of fun.

Jimmy said, "Can we play at your house
next time, Peter?
I want to see your frog."

"All right," said Peter.
"But come without your cat.
Don't forget.
Frogs don't like cats."

After that the three boys had lots of fun.
Sometimes they played at Peter's house.
Sometimes they went to Edward's house.
And sometimes they went to Jimmy's house.

People said, "Edward and Peter
and Jimmy are like brothers."

And they were!

Friends of the Neighborhood

Your teacher will read this to you.

The place where you live is your *neighborhood*. There are all kinds of neighborhoods. Some are in the city. Some are in the country. Some are large. Some are small. Large or small, every neighborhood has friends.

Do you know these friends?

These friends are police officers. They help keep your neighborhood safe.

Clang! There's a fire on Main Street! These friends rush to put the fire out. They are both good firefighters.

Someone has written you a letter. This friend brings it to your home. He is a mail carrier.

Does your neighborhood have busy streets? Be sure to look both ways before you cross! On some streets, there are friends to help you. This woman is a school crossing guard. The boy is a member of the school safety patrol.

Who are some of the other friends in your neighborhood? Do they help make your neighborhood a good place to live?

That's What Friends Are For

Florence Parry Heide and Sylvia Worth Van Clief

Teddy has a bad leg.
And this is the day he was going
to see his cousin!

"What can I do?" Teddy asks.
"I can't go to my cousin's now.
I can't walk on my bad leg.
I'll ask my friends.
They will tell me what to do.
That's what friends are for," says Teddy.

Then Teddy's friend the bird comes by.
"What are you doing here?"
asks the bird.

"I have a bad leg, and I can't walk.
And I can't go to see my cousin,"
says Teddy.

"If I had a bad leg," says the bird,
"I would fly to see my cousin."

"Thank you for telling me
what to do," says Teddy.

"That's what friends are for,"
says the bird.

Then Teddy's friend the daddy-longlegs
comes by.

"What are you doing here?"
asks the daddy-longlegs.

"I have a bad leg and I can't walk.
And I can't fly.
And I can't go to see my cousin,"
says Teddy.

"If I had a bad leg,"
says the daddy-longlegs,
"I would walk.
I have lots of legs."

"Thank you for telling me
what to do," says Teddy.

"That's what friends are for,"
says the daddy-longlegs.

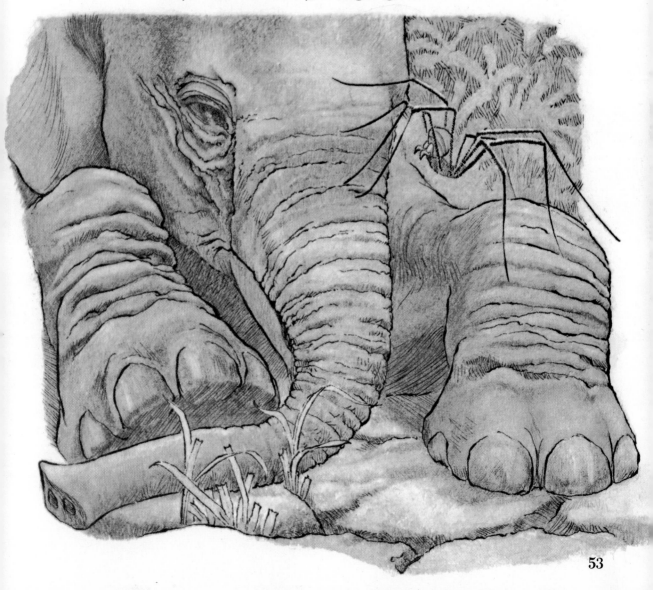

Then Teddy's friend the monkey
comes by.

"What are you doing here?"
asks the monkey.

"I have a bad leg, and I can't walk.
And I can't fly.
And I don't have lots of legs.
And I can't go to see my cousin,"
says Teddy.

"If I had a bad leg," says the monkey,
"I would go from tree to tree like this."

"Thank you for telling me what to do,"
says Teddy.

"That's what friends are for,"
says the monkey.

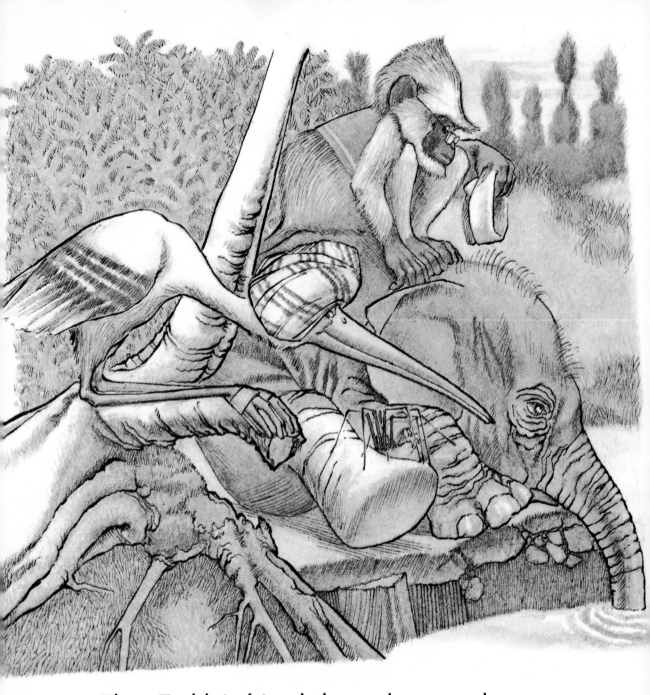

Then Teddy's friend the crab comes by.

"What are you doing here?"
asks the crab.

"I have a bad leg, and I can't walk.
And I can't fly.
And I don't have lots of legs.
And I can't go from tree to tree
by my tail.
And I can't go to see my cousin,"
says Teddy.

"If I had a bad leg," says the crab,
"I would get a new one."

"Thank you for telling me
what to do," says Teddy.

"That's what friends are for,"
says the crab.

Then Teddy's friend the raccoon
comes by.

"What is all the noise?" he asks.

"Teddy has a bad leg," says the bird.
"He can't fly."

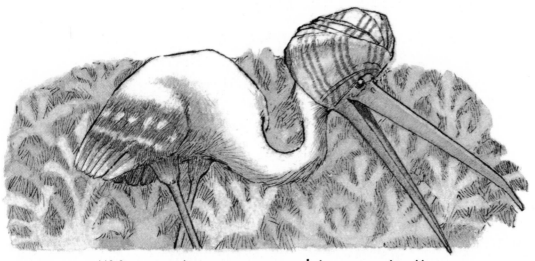

"He can't go to see his cousin,"
says the crab.

"We are telling him what to do,"
says the monkey.

"That's what friends are for,"
says the daddy-longlegs.

"No," says the raccoon.
"Friends are to help!"

"Help?" asks the bird.

"Yes," says the raccoon.
"You can help Teddy.
Go and get his cousin.
Tell him to come here to see Teddy."

All the friends go to find
Teddy's cousin.
When they come back,
Teddy's cousin is with them.

"Thank you for helping me,"
says Teddy.

61

To give advice is very nice,
but friends can do much more.
Friends should always help a friend.
That's what friends are for!

—Florence Parry Heide
Sylvia Worth Van Clief

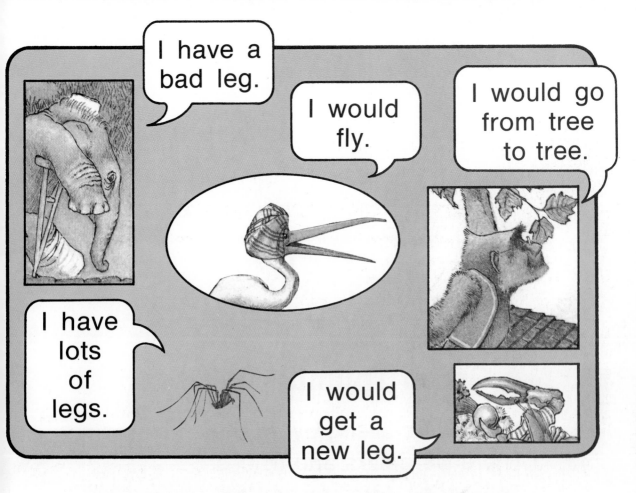

What Did You Say?

"I have a bad leg," said Teddy.

"I would fly," said the bird.

"I would go from tree to tree," said the monkey.

"I have lots of legs," said the daddy-longlegs.

"I would get a new leg," said the crab.

Punctuation Cues. Have the children read what each animal is saying in the illustrations. Then have them find the sentence below that tells what the animal said. Note how the animals' words are placed in balloons in illustrations and between quotation marks in sentences.

The Little Red Flower
Paul Tripp

PART ONE

A Green Thumb

No flowers ever grew in the small town.
There were cars and trucks.
There were lots of people.
But there were no flowers.

One day Mr. Greenthumb came to town.
He came with a little red flower.
He put the flower in his window.

Boys and girls walked by
Mr. Greenthumb's house.
They saw the red flower.
And they stopped to look at it.

"What is it?"

"It looks like a flower."

"It looks like a picture
I saw in a book."

The next morning lots of people came
to see the flower.

"My boy was right," said a mother.
"It **is** a flower."

The people saw Mr. Greenthumb open
his window.
They saw him put water on his flower.

"Did you see that?" asked a man.
"His thumb is green."

"That's right," said a woman.
"That's what you have to have
to grow flowers."

Mr. Greenthumb looked up
and saw all the people.

"Good morning," said a man.
"We came to see your flower.
We can't get flowers to grow
in this town."

"That's too bad," said Mr. Greenthumb.
"Would you all like to smell my flower?"

"Yes," said the people.

One by one they went up to the window.
They all loved the smell of the flower.

Every morning was like that.
People would come to Mr.
Greenthumb's house.
They would see him water the flower.
One by one they would walk to the window.
They would smell the flower.
They would say, "M-m-m.
That flower smells good."
One by one they would walk home.

All people thought about was the flower.
Every man thought about it.
Every woman thought about it.
Every boy and girl thought about it.
Some of them made pictures of it.
One girl made lots of signs.
The signs said, "To the flower."
She put the signs on every street in town.

PART TWO

Who Can Save the Flower?

One morning Mr. Greenthumb
did not come to the window.

"Where is he?" asked a boy.

"I'll find out," said a man.
"I'll find him and talk to him.
You wait here."

All the people waited.
The man went
into Mr. Greenthumb's house.
Then he came out of the house.

"Where is the doctor?
Mr. Greenthumb is sick!" he said.

"The doctor went to the school,"
said a woman.
"He is still there."

The man ran to the school.
He got the doctor.
They went back
to Mr. Greenthumb's house.

The people were still waiting
at Mr. Greenthumb's house.
They saw the doctor go in.
They waited all morning.
He did not come out.
They waited all afternoon.
Still he did not come out.

Night came.
The doctor opened the door.
"Mr. Greenthumb is very sick,"
he said.
"He will be all right.
But his flower may not be.
Who will save it?"

The people looked at the flower.
It looked sick, too.

"You are a doctor," said a man.
"Can't you help the little red flower?"

"No," said the doctor.
"I'm a people doctor,
not a flower doctor.
One of **you** will have to save
Mr. Greenthumb's flower."

The doctor went back
into the house.

74

"Who can save the red flower?"
asked a woman.

"Who has a green thumb?" asked a man.

"Let me try," said a boy.
"I can do it.
I can save the little flower."

"You can't save it!" said a man.
"You don't have a green thumb."

"Let him try," said a woman.

"Yes! Let him try,"
said all the people.

That night the doctor sat
by Mr. Greenthumb's bed.
All night he sat there.
The boy sat by the red flower.
He put water on the flower.
Then he went to sleep.

PART THREE
New Flowers

Day after day the boy sat
by the flower.
People came by the house.
They looked at the flower.
They waited for Mr. Greenthumb.
He still did not come out.
They still did not see him.
So they went home.

77

One day the people came
to Mr. Greenthumb's house.
They saw the door open.
They saw the doctor come out.
Mr. Greenthumb was with him.
It was good to see him again.

The people were happy.
And Mr. Greenthumb was happy.
He was happy to be out of bed.
He was happy to be with friends, too.

Then the boy came out.
He had the little red flower with him.

"Look!" said the boy.
"I did save the flower."

"He did it without a green thumb,"
said a man.

"Mr. Greenthumb," said the boy,
"look at your thumb.
It isn't green.
We thought you had a green thumb."

Mr. Greenthumb looked down at his thumb.
"The paint is gone," he said.

"What paint?" asked a man.

"I had green paint on my thumb,"
said Mr. Greenthumb.

All the people laughed.

"All right!" said Mr. Greenthumb.
"You don't have to have a green thumb
to grow flowers.
Who wants to try to grow a flower?
I have seeds for all of you."

The boys and girls wanted to try.
Every one of them got the seeds.

The boys and girls put water
on their seeds every day.
Then they waited for their seeds
to grow.

And in time their seeds did grow.

Now, thanks to Mr. Greenthumb,
there is a little red flower
in every window in town.

At Mrs. Appleby's

When frost is shining on the trees,
  It's spring at Mrs. Appleby's.
You smell it in the air before
  You step inside the kitchen door.

Rows of scarlet flowers bloom
  From every window in the room.
And funny little speckled fish
  Are swimming in a china dish.

A tiny bird with yellow wings
  Just sits and sings and sings and SINGS!
Outside when frost is on the trees,
  It's spring at Mrs. Appleby's.

—Elizabeth Upham McWebb

Two Into One

Let us go to the carnival.
Let's go to the carnival.

That is Peter's puppy.
That's Peter's puppy.

The store is not open.
The store isn't open.

We are playing a new game.
We're playing a new game.

Contractions. Discuss the illustrations. Note the two words at the beginning of each set and one word at the end. Call attention to the missing letters and the use of the apostrophe. Have the sentences under the illustrations read.

ALL KINDS OF FAMILIES

André

—Gwendolyn Brooks

I had a dream last night. I dreamed
I had to pick a mother out.
I had to choose a father too.
At first, I wondered what to do,
There were so many there, it seemed,
Short and tall and thin and stout.

But just before I sprang awake,
I knew what parents I would take.
And *this* surprised and made me glad:
They were the ones I always had!

Maggie in the Middle

Judy Blume

PART ONE

The Middle Is No Place To Be

Maggie had a big sister, Ellen.
She had a little brother, Mike.
Maggie was the one in the middle.
And she didn't like it.
But what could she do?

Ellen got too big for her clothes.
Ellen's old clothes fit Maggie.
Maggie got the old clothes.
Ellen got new ones.

At one time Maggie had her own room.
Then Mike came.
Mike had to have a room of his own.
And Maggie had to sleep in Ellen's room.

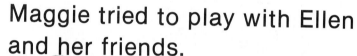

Maggie tried to play with Ellen
and her friends.

But Ellen said, "Go away, Maggie.
Run and play with your own friends.
This is not a game for little girls."

Maggie tried to play with Mike.
It was no fun.
Mike would not play right.
He ran away with Maggie's games.
He put them in his room.

Maggie's mother came
into the room.

"Mike won't play right," said Maggie.
"He ran away with my games."

"Mike is too little to play with you,"
said Mother.
"Let him play with his own games."

Maggie was too big for Mike.
She was too little for Ellen.
Maggie was in the middle.

"The middle!" thought Maggie.
"That's no place to be."

PART TWO

Maggie Gets a Part

One noon Maggie saw a sign in school.
The sign said,

"That's for me," said Maggie.
I'll ask Mrs. Cook
if I can have a part in the play."

Maggie ran to her room.

"Mrs. Cook," said Maggie.
"I want to be in the school play."

"The play is for big boys and girls,"
said Mrs. Cook.

"I see," said Maggie.
She looked down.
"Big girls like Ellen."

Maggie walked out of the room.

94

The next morning Mrs. Cook
had news for Maggie.
She waited for Maggie to come
into the room.

Then she said,
"Mrs. Chang wants to see you, Maggie.
She may have a part for you
in the school play."

"Thanks!" said Maggie.

At noon Maggie went
to see Mrs. Chang.

"I'm Maggie," she said.
"I want to be in the play."

"Say it on the stage," said Mrs. Chang.

Maggie went up on the stage.
The stage was very big.
Maggie looked very little.

"I'M MAGGIE," she said.
"I WANT TO BE IN THE PLAY."

"Good," said Mrs. Chang.
"Now, can you jump?"

"Can I **jump**?" said Maggie.

Maggie did big jumps.

Then she did little jumps.

Then she did big jumps again.

Maggie could jump all right.

"Good, Maggie," said Mrs. Chang.
"You will make a good kangaroo."

"**Kangaroo** !" said Maggie.

"A green kangaroo," said Mrs. Chang.
"Your part in the play will be
the Green Kangaroo."

PART THREE
The One in the Middle Is the Green Kangaroo

After school, Maggie didn't talk
about the play.
She waited for everyone to sit down to eat.
Then she said, "I got a part
in the school play.
I'm going to be the Green Kangaroo."

The **Green** Kangaroo!" said Ellen. She laughed
at the thought of a **green** kangaroo.

"That's right," said Maggie.
"I'm going to be the **Green** Kangaroo."

Everyone laughed.
"Good for you, Maggie," said Mother.
And Daddy said, "I'm so happy for you."

Maggie worked on her kangaroo jumps every day.
She did kangaroo jumps on the stage at school.
She did them at home.

One night Ellen came into the room.
She saw Maggie jumping on the bed.

"What are you doing?" asked Ellen.

"I'm the Green Kangaroo!" called Maggie.

Then the day of the play came.
Maggie went to Mrs. Chang's room.
Mrs. Chang helped Maggie get
into her kangaroo clothes.

Maggie jumped all over the room.

"I'm the Green Kangaroo," she called.

The boys and girls laughed.
And so did Mrs. Chang.

It was time for the play.
Maggie jumped out on the stage.
Lots of people were at the play.
Maggie's mother and daddy were there.
So were Mike and Ellen.
They were in the middle of all the people.
Maggie wasn't in the middle!
She was alone on the stage.

"Hello,"

called Maggie.

"I'm the Green Kangaroo."

The play went on.
Maggie did her little jumps.
She jumped all over the stage.

Someone would ask,
"And who are you?"

Maggie would say,

"I'm the Green Kangaroo."

When Maggie said that,
everyone would laugh.
Maggie liked it when they laughed.

Then the play was over.
The boys and girls came out
on the stage.

Mrs. Chang came out and said,
"I want to thank Maggie.
She played the part of the Green Kangaroo."

Maggie jumped on the stage.
She jumped to the middle of the stage.

Everyone liked Maggie.
It was Maggie's big day.

After that, Maggie didn't care
if she got Ellen's old clothes.
She didn't care
that she didn't have her own room.
She didn't care
that she was the one in the middle.
Being Maggie wasn't so bad after all.

Just About

I'm just about ready
   To turn to a gnome.
I'm tired of staying
   So close to home.

I'm just about ready
   to turn to an elf.
I'm quite tired of being
   Only myself.

I'm just about ready
   To turn to a sprite,
But I'll be myself, home again,
   Long before night.

—Leland B. Jacobs

Short Cut

Mr. Bob's Button Co.

Park Ave.
Green St.

Dr. Brown

Mrs. Baker's Tea Room
open Mon.-Sat.

Abbreviations. Have children find abbreviations in the street scene. Write the unabbreviated words and the abbreviations on the board for comparison. Point out use of capital letters and periods in these abbreviations.

The New Spring Hats

PART ONE

Eleanor Clymer

Hats Everywhere

It was spring.
Birds were singing.
Flowers were everywhere.
All the people had on new spring hats.

"I would like a new spring hat, too,"
Belinda said to her mother and daddy.

"You would?" asked Mother.
"We'll get one for you."

"When?" asked Belinda.

"Soon," said Mother.
"But we can't get one for you now.
You will have to wait."

Belinda waited.
All the time she was playing
and going to school, she waited.

One day Belinda said,
"I'll have to find my own hat."

So Belinda looked all over the house.
Then she saw a good hat.
She put it on her head
and went to show her mother.

"Belinda!" said Mother.
"What is that on your head?"

"It's my new spring hat,"
said Belinda.
"Do you like it?"

"Very much," said her mother.
"But it looks a little like a bowl."

Belinda looked in the mirror.
Her spring hat did look like a bowl.
So she put it back
and went to find another one.

"Here is a good hat," she said.

She put it on and went to show
her aunt.

"Hello, Belinda," said her aunt.
"What is that on your head?"

"It's my new spring hat,"
said Belinda.
"Is it all right?"

"Yes it is," said Belinda's aunt.
"I like it very much.
But isn't it too big?"

Belinda tried to look in the mirror.
But she couldn't see.
Her aunt was right.

"This hat is much too big for me,"
said Belinda.

So she put it on the floor
and went to find another hat.

PART TWO
Belinda's Hat

Belinda found another hat.
She liked this one very much.
She put it on and went to
show Grandma.

"Belinda," said Grandma.
"What is that on your head?"

"It's my new spring hat,"
said Belinda.
"I found it.
Do you like it?"

"I do," said Grandma.
"But it looks a little like
the box the cat sleeps in."

Belinda looked in the mirror.

"You are right, Grandma," she said.
"I can't wear this."

Belinda put the box back on the
floor, and the cat got into it.

Belinda walked out of the house.

"I have to find a hat to wear
for spring," she said.
"Maybe I'll find one out here."

By the time her daddy came home,
Belinda had found a new hat.

"Hello, Belinda," said Daddy.
"What is that on your head?"

"It's my new spring hat,"
said Belinda.
"Do you like it?"

"Yes," said her daddy.
"There won't be another girl
in town with a hat like that."

Belinda laughed.

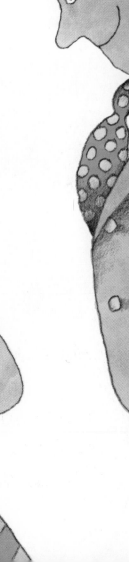

"What have you got there, Daddy?"
Belinda asked.

"This is a plant for Mother.
Would you like to help me put
it in a flower pot?" asked Daddy.

"Yes," said Belinda.
"But where is the flower pot?"

"It's in the box," said Daddy.
"Open it."

Belinda opened the box.

"What is this?" she asked.

"It's the flower pot," said Daddy.

"Daddy," said Belinda.
"You can't put the plant in that!"

"No," said Daddy.
"Maybe you are right.
But what will we do with the plant?
I can't get another flower pot now." 119

"Take my hat," said Belinda.

"All right," said Daddy.
"But you will have to wear
the flower pot."

"I would love to," said Belinda.

And she went to show her mother,
her aunt, and her grandma
her new spring hat.

MR. SPATS

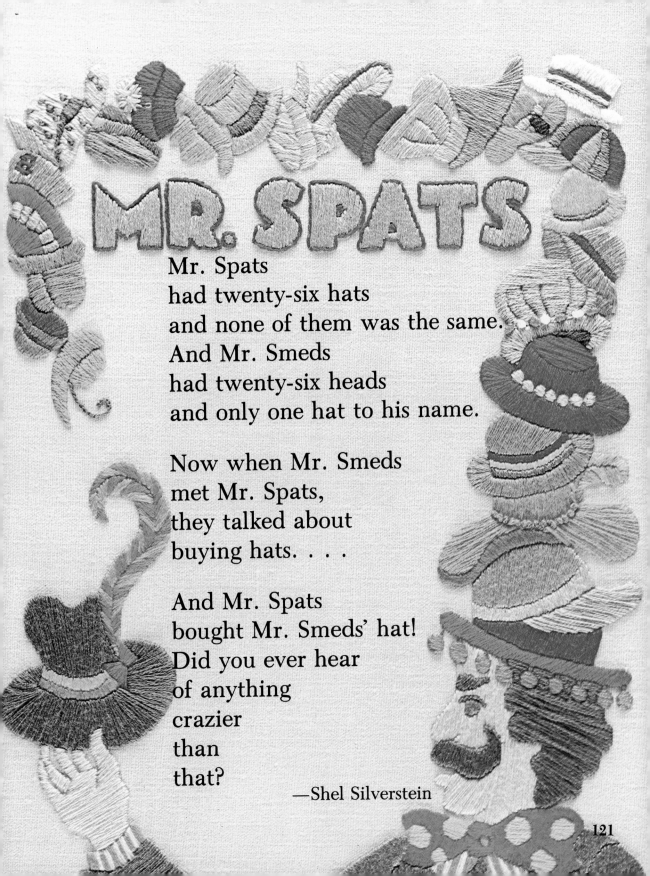

Mr. Spats
had twenty-six hats
and none of them was the same.
And Mr. Smeds
had twenty-six heads
and only one hat to his name.

Now when Mr. Smeds
met Mr. Spats,
they talked about
buying hats. . . .

And Mr. Spats
bought Mr. Smeds' hat!
Did you ever hear
of anything
crazier
than
that?

—Shel Silverstein

Friends of the Family

Many workers perform *services* for other people. This means that they *do things* for other people. And that's being a friend!

Have the lights ever gone out in your home? What did your family do? Did you call an electrician? This friend is an electrician. She knows how to put in electric wiring and repair it.

Has your kitchen sink ever had a leaky faucet? Or clogged pipes? This friend is a plumber. He knows how to repair the pipes and faucets in your home.

This friend works for a telephone company. Her job is to install phones in homes and offices.

This friend is performing a very special service in the home. She is a clothing designer. She is helping a mother choose the cloth for a new suit. Today, many people make use of shop-at-home services.

What are some of the services that your family uses?

Liesel Moak Skorpen

All the Lassies

PART ONE
Just One Wish

"I wish I had a dog," said Peter.

"I know you do," said his mother.
"But we don't have room for a dog."

"Just a little dog," said Peter.

"No," said his mother.
"How about a fish?"

Peter named his fish Lassie.
He tried to make the fish come to
him when he called.

"Here, Lassie," called Peter.
"Here, Lassie, old girl."

But the fish didn't come.

"I would like a dog," said Peter.

"I know you would," said his mother, "but we don't have room for a dog."

"Just a little one?" asked Peter.

"No," said his mother, "but you can have a turtle."

125

Peter named his turtle **Lassie.**
He wanted the turtle to wag its tail.
All morning Peter tried to make
the turtle wag its tail.

"Come on, Lassie," said Peter.
"Wag your tail."

But the turtle didn't wag its tail.

"I wish I had a dog," said Peter.

"Don't you like your turtle?"
asked his mother.

"I like it very much," said Peter.
"I just wish I had a dog."

"I know," said his mother.
"How would you like a bird?"

Peter named his bird Lassie.
He tried to make the bird say,
"Woof, woof."
But all the bird could say was,

"Tweet, tweet."

PART TWO

All the Lassies and Walter

"I wish I had a dog," said Peter.

"I know you do," said his mother.
"But we don't have room for a dog."

"All I want is a little dog," said Peter.

"I know someone who has two kittens,"
said his mother.
"How would you like a kitten?"

Peter named his kitten Lassie.
"I'll throw the ball, Lassie.
You bring it back to me," said Peter.

The kitten saw Peter throw the ball.
The kitten ran to get the ball.
But she didn't bring it back to Peter.

"You are a good kitten," said Peter.
"But you are not a good dog."

That night Peter's mother came into his room to say good night.

"Mother," said Peter.
"I would like to have a dog."

"All right," said his mother.
"You may have a very little dog."

The next day Peter and his mother went
to the pet store.
They came home with a very big dog.
The dog came when Peter called him.
He could wag his tail.
He could say,

"WOOF,
WOOF."

When Peter would throw the ball,
the dog would bring it back.

Peter named the dog **WALTER.**
Walter made very good friends
with all the Lassies.

Bert's Berries

George McCue

PART ONE

Bert

Big Bert liked to eat.
All bears do.
But Bert was not like
any other bear.
Bert liked to eat berries.
Not fish!
Not what other bears eat!
Just berries!

But in winter it was cold.
It was too cold for berries.
So Bert sat in his cave.
He thought about berries.

All the other bears went to sleep.
They would sleep all winter.
But not Bert!
He sat in the cold cave.
He thought about berries.

One day winter was over.
Bert ran from his cave.

"It's time for berries again!" he said.

Bert found some berries.
But they were too green to eat.
So he waited.
Every day he went to look at the berries.

One day he said,
"The berries look good.
They are not so green.
Any day now I can eat them."

There was no sleep for Bert that night.
He thought about all the berries.
He would eat them in the morning.

When morning came, Bert ran to the berries.
But what did he find?
Some of his berries were gone!

"Who would do that?" Bert thought.
"Who would eat my berries?"

There were lots of berries for Bert.
But he didn't care.
He didn't want lots of berries.
He wanted **all** the berries!

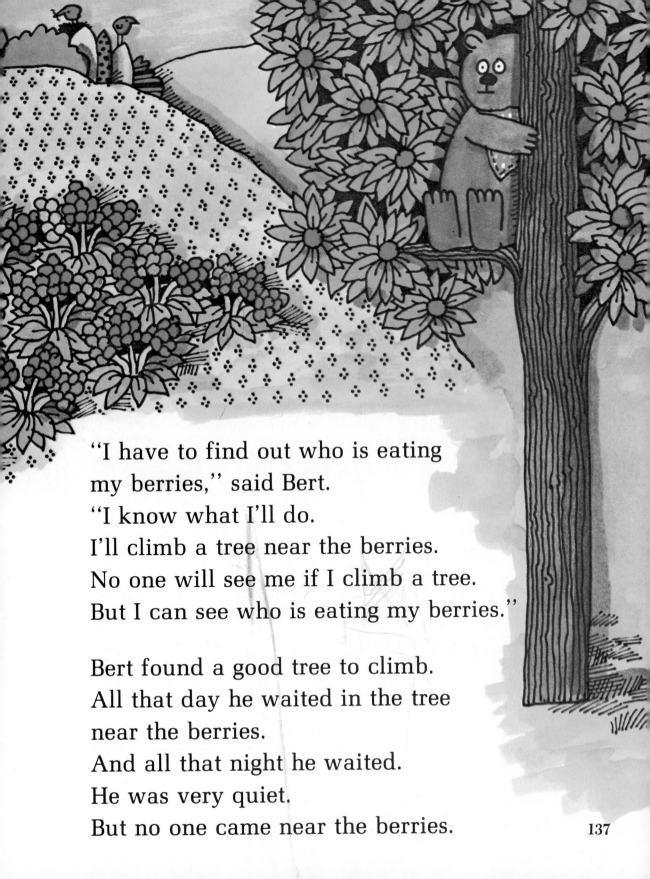

"I have to find out who is eating
my berries," said Bert.
"I know what I'll do.
I'll climb a tree near the berries.
No one will see me if I climb a tree.
But I can see who is eating my berries."

Bert found a good tree to climb.
All that day he waited in the tree
near the berries.
And all that night he waited.
He was very quiet.
But no one came near the berries.

PART TWO
A Happy Bear

The next day Bert saw a fox.
The fox was near the berries.
He began to eat Bert's berries.

"Stop it! Stop it!" called Bert.

138

The fox looked up in the tree
and saw Big Bert.

"Why do you want me to stop?"
he asked.
"I don't eat very much.
Why can't I have some of the berries?"

"Because I want them all," said Big Bert.
"Now get out of there.
I won't let you eat my berries."

"If I go, the rabbits will come,"
said the fox.

"And then you will have no berries at all."

Bert began to laugh.
"There are no rabbits here," he said.

"That's right," said the fox.
"There are no rabbits here now.
That's because they know I'll eat them.
If I go, the rabbits will come.
They will eat the berries."

Bert laughed at the fox again.

"The rabbits won't come here," said Bert.
"Now get out of here.
Don't let me see you
near my berries again."

And so the fox had to go.

Bert was very happy.
He was happy because he had
all the berries.
Then he saw a rabbit.
Then two rabbits!
Then three!
There were rabbits all over the place.
They were eating his berries!

"Stop it! Stop it!" called Bert.

The rabbits went right on eating.
Bert ran after them.
But he couldn't get near the rabbits.
He couldn't run like they could.
He tried and tried.
But he didn't get one rabbit.
He had to stop and sit down.

The rabbits began to laugh at Bert.
And that did not make Bert a happy bear.

"What can I do?" thought Bert.
"I know," he said.
"I will go and find the fox."
And that's what he did.

"Fox," said Bert, "come back with me.
You can have some of my berries."

"Why do you want me now?"
asked the fox.

"Because you were right," said Bert.
"The rabbits did come.
They will eat all the berries
if you don't stop them.
Will you come back?" asked Bert.

"Thank you," said the fox.
"I will."

He went back to the berries.

When the rabbits saw the fox, they ran.
They didn't come back again.

The fox had all the berries he wanted.
Bert had all the berries he wanted.
Now Bert could laugh at the rabbits.
He was a very happy bear.

The Family in Art

The family is found in many great works of art.
Each artist shows the family in a different way.

CHESTER DALE COLLECTION. NATIONAL GALLERY OF ART, WASHINGTON, D.C.

The Boating Party

MARY CASSATT

Mary Cassatt painted this picture of a family
having fun together. She shows you how they feel
by the way they are looking at each other.

CHARLES WHITE, *IMAGES OF DIGNITY*, THE WARD RITCHIE PRESS

Mother and Child

CHARLES WHITE

Charles White drew this picture with a pencil.
He made the faces and hands of the mother and
her baby the most important part of the picture.
Can you see how he did it?

146

Don Doll took this photograph of a very old man holding a very young child. How do you think they feel about each other?

Leo Makes Room for Them, with Rocky

DON DOLL, S. J.

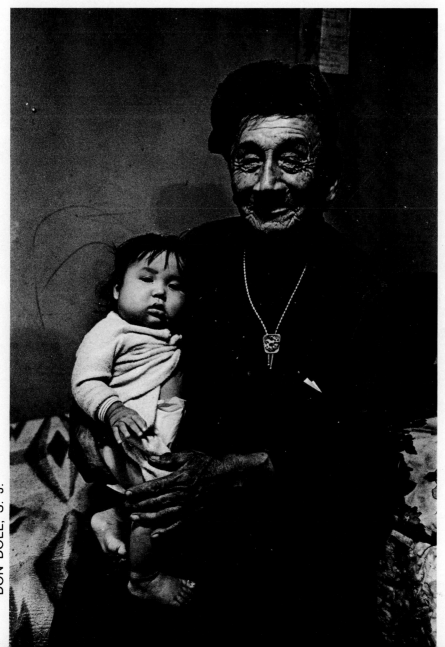

DON DOLL, S. J.

147

Renoir painted this portrait of a mother and her two little girls. A portrait looks just like a picture taken with a camera. The artist paints the people the way they really look. Even the dog got into this family portrait.

Madame Charpentier and Her Children

PIERRE AUGUSTE RENOIR

Rocking Chair No. 2

HENRY MOORE

Henry Moore made this metal sculpture of a mother rocking her baby. Notice how smooth and rounded he made them. That's the way this artist likes to work.

LINDA FERRAN, BROOKLYN, NEW YORK

An artist in the first grade did this crayon drawing
of her family. Some grown-up artists use
crayons, too.

Isi and His Sons

An Egyptian artist carved a father and his sons
in a huge block of stone. He made the father much
bigger than his sons to show how important he was.

KAZIMIERZ MICHALOWSKI, *L'ART DE L'ANCIENNE EGYPTE*, EDITIONS D'ART
LUCIEN MAZENOD, PARIS

151

The Walk to Paradise Garden

W. EUGENE SMITH

A photographer took this picture of his children
when they were walking in the woods one day.
You can't see their faces, but can you tell how they
feel about each other?

A Quiet Walk

When I take Peg to walk,
We hardly ever talk.
There's just too much to see.
I like to laugh and play,
But—somehow—not today.
And Peg feels just like me.
We're quiet when we walk
For we don't need to talk.
There's just too much to see.

—Pete Shiflet

153

1 bear
bears

2 fox
foxes

3 berry
berries

One or More?

Get that <u>fly</u> out of here!
Frogs and fish eat <u>flies</u>.

A <u>rabbit</u> lives near the tree.
The <u>rabbits</u> live near the tree.

Look at the <u>puppy</u>. I have one <u>wish</u>.
Look at the <u>puppies</u>. You have two <u>wishes</u>.

Plural Forms. Have the numbered pairs of words read. Point out how the plural for each pair was formed. Have the sentences read. Have the children decide if the plurals of the underlined words were formed as in 1, 2, or 3. Then have the children create similar sentences using the singular and plural forms of *lady, ball, box,* and *bunny.*

Three Guesses

hat
hit
hot

bad   bed   bud

leg   log   lag

fin   fan   fun

pet
pat
pot

net
not
nut

Medial Vowel Substitution. Have the three words in each box read. Ask which word goes with the picture.

ALL KINDS OF PLACES TO GO

How to Tell the Top of a Hill

The top of a hill
  Is not until
The bottom is below.
And you have to stop
When you reach the top
For there's no more UP to go.

To make it plain
Let me explain:
The one most reason why
You have to stop
When you reach the top—is:
The next step up is sky.   —John Ciardi

A Place for Carmen

Carmen wanted to go somewhere.
She didn't know **where.**
But she wanted to go somewhere.

Daddy went places.
Mother went places, too.
Every day they went into the big city.
Mother and Daddy worked in the city.

Rosa went lots of places.
Rosa was Carmen's big sister.
She had her own car.

"I'd go lots of places," thought Carmen,
"if I had my own car!"

Grandma lived with Carmen's family.
She took care of Carmen after school.
She took care of Pablo, too.
Pablo was Carmen's little brother.

Grandma went places on Sundays.
Grandma went to the country.
Carmen's aunt lived in the country.
Every Sunday Grandma went to see her.
"I'm the only one who never goes places!"
thought Carmen.

One day Carmen asked Grandma about it.

"Mother and Daddy go places," she said.
"Rosa goes places.
I'm the only one who never goes places.
Why is that?"

"The **only** one?" asked Grandma.
Grandma looked at Pablo.

"Maybe not the **only** one," said Carmen.
"But Pablo is too little.
He **can't** go anywhere!"

"I wouldn't say that," said Grandma.
"Pablo could go with you . . .
if you went somewhere."

"Yes, **if** I went somewhere," said
Carmen.

Grandma said, "Why don't you ask
about it?
Why don't you ask Daddy and Mother?"

That night Carmen did as Grandma said.
She asked her family if she could go
somewhere.

"Will next Sunday be all right?"
Daddy asked.

"Yes!" said Carmen.

Mother asked, "Where do you want to go?"

"I don't know yet," said Carmen.
"I'll have to think of a special place."

Carmen began to think of a place to go.
She thought about the big city.
Carmen had a picture book about the city.
She looked at the pictures in it.
She saw lots of places to go.

Pablo saw Carmen looking at the pictures.
"Read me a story," he said.
"Please, Carmen."

Carmen put the picture book away.
She got out one of Pablo's books.
She read him a story.
It was about a kangaroo.
Carmen showed her brother pictures
of the kangaroo.

"I wish I could see a **real** kangaroo,"
said Pablo.

The next day Carmen thought again
about where to go.
This time she thought about the country.
"What's it like in the country?" she asked
Grandma.

"Oh, it's nice!" said Grandma.
"Very nice!
Lots of trees grow in the country.
And there are lots of animals!"

"Are there bears?" asked Carmen.

"No," said Grandma.
"There aren't
any bears!"

"Bears!" said Pablo.
He ran to get his toy bear.
"Play with me," he said.
"Please play with me and my bear."

Carmen played with her brother and his bear.

"I wish I could see a **real** bear!"
her brother said.

165

The next day Carmen thought,
"I want to think of a **very** special place to go."
Then she thought of the park.

The park was a nice place.
Maybe she could take a friend to the park.
Maybe Rosa would take them there in her car.

Carmen got out her paints.
She would make a picture of the park.
She would put Rosa's car in the picture.
She would show the picture to her family.
Then they would know where she wanted to go.

Pablo saw Carmen get out her paints.
"Paint me a picture," he said.
"Paint me a picture of a tiger.
Please, Carmen."

Carmen painted a picture for her brother.
It was a picture of a big tiger.

"I wish I could see a **real** tiger," said
Pablo.

That night Carmen's family was at home.

Daddy said, "Sunday is coming, Carmen.
Have you thought about where you want
to go?"

"If you have, tell us," said Rosa.

"Yes, tell us," said Mother.

Carmen didn't know what to say.
She had thought about some places to go.
But they were not very special places.

Carmen looked at Daddy.
He was waiting.
She looked at Mother and Rosa.
They were waiting, too.

Then Carmen looked at her little brother.
"I know where I want to go!" she said.
"I know of a very special place.
It's a place that has real kangaroos!
And bears! And tigers!
I want to go to the zoo!"

So that's where Carmen went on Sunday.
Pablo went, too.
So did Grandma,
and Mother,
and Daddy,
and Rosa!
The zoo was a special place for them, too.

New Neighbors

When Smiths packed up
and moved away,
and Judy was gone,
I cried all day.

I knew I'd never
like anyone
as much as Judy
or have such fun.

Then Browns moved in
with a silky cat
and a dog with puppies.
Imagine that!

And a girl named Becky . . .
and I forgot
all about missing
Judy a lot.

—Aileen Fisher

The Browns Say Good-by

PART ONE
Moving Day

The Browns were moving.
They were moving to a new town.
The moving truck had not come.
The Browns were waiting for it.
Mrs. Brown was putting clothes into a box.
Mr. Brown was putting boxes into a car.

Bobby had gone down the street
to say good-by to his friends.
He gave his goldfish
to his friend Jay.
He gave his turtle
to his friend Ben.
And he gave his frog
to his friend Mike.

At last Bobby got home.
People who lived on his street came by.
They came to say a last good-by.
Mrs. O'Hara came with cookies.
They were for Bobby and his sister, Jenny.
Mr. Green came with some seeds.
They were for Bobby.

Just then the moving truck came.
Men began putting boxes into the truck.
At last it was time to go.
Bobby didn't want to go to a new town.
He ran to the big tree
in back of the house.
He climbed up.
Bobby's father ran after him.
"Bobby," called his father.
"It's time to go."

"I'm not going," said Bobby.
"I won't have any friends.
And there won't be any trees to climb.
And I don't want to go to a new school."

"I saw lots of boys and girls
for you to play with," said his father.
"There's a school just down the street
from the new house.
And there's a big tree right
in back of the house."

Bobby climbed down from the tree.
He walked to the car with his father.

"I'll take a look
at the new house," said Bobby.
"But I'm not going to live there.
I don't want to live in any house
but this one."

Bobby was not happy about moving.
But he got into the car.
He looked out the window
at the house and the big tree.
The moving truck had gone.
The Browns were off to their
new home.

PART TWO
The New House

Soon the Browns reached their new house.

Bobby and Jenny got out of the car.

They ran into the house.

They opened all the doors.

They looked in all the rooms.

All the rooms smelled of new paint.

Jenny found a good place
in her room for her toys.
Mrs. Brown came in to help her
take them out of the boxes.
Then she went into Bobby's room.

"Do you like your room, Bobby?"
asked Mrs. Brown.

"It's a good room," said Bobby.
"But it's not like my old room.
I'll sleep here tonight.
Then I'm moving back
to our old house."

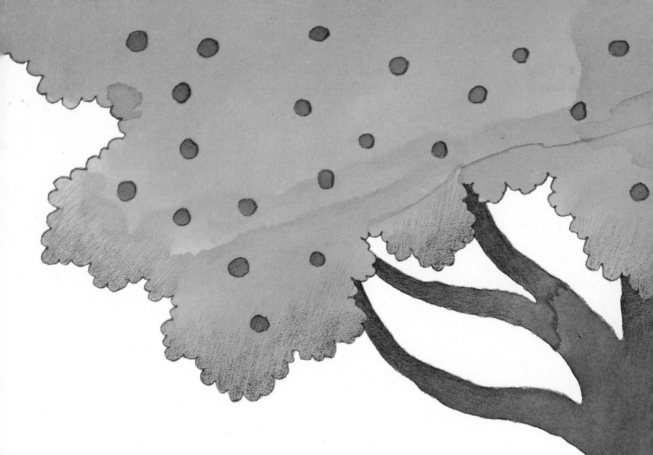

Bobby looked out the bedroom window
and saw a big tree.

"That looks like a good tree,"
he said to his mother.
"But it's not like the tree
back at our old house.
It's just not the same.
There's no treehouse in this one.
I'll climb the tree in the morning,
just to see what it's like.
But then I'm going back to my old tree."

The next morning Bobby was playing
in the big tree.
Two boys came by.
They stopped when they saw him.

"What are you doing up in that tree?"
asked one of the boys.
"That's our tree."

"No it isn't," said Bobby.
"It's my tree now.
It came with the house.
That's my house, and this is my tree."

"Come on, Dan," said one boy.
"We can find another tree."

The two boys began to walk
up the street.

"Wait!" said Bobby.
"There's room for you in the tree.
Climb up."

So the two boys climbed up the tree.
And the three boys played games
182   in the tree all morning.

Jenny soon found her own friends.
One friend had lots of hats.
Jenny loved hats.
She couldn't wait to try them on.
Another friend had some kittens.
One day Jenny tried on hats.
Another day she played with the kittens.
Jenny was happy in the new house.

That night Bobby's father came
into his room.

"Do you want to go back
to our old house?" he asked.
"I'll take you back tonight."

"No," said Bobby.
"I thought it over.
I have lots of work to do here.
Mr. Green gave me some seeds to plant.
I have to plant my seeds.
I have to make a treehouse.
I have to get some new pets.
My pets may like my new room.
If they do, I may live here."

The next day Bobby began to plant his seeds.
He began to make a treehouse.
It soon looked the same as his old one.
Bobby's friends helped him to find some pets.
His room soon looked the same as the old one.
As Bobby thought about it, the new house
was not so bad.

People on the Go

Some people work in their own neighborhoods. Other people must travel to get to their jobs. They go by car, by bus, by train, or by subway. Some people even go by plane!

People on the go need friends.

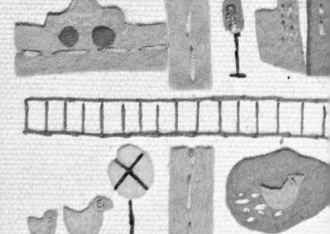

This friend is a train engineer. He has worked on the railroad for many years. His job is to run the train.

This man owns his own taxicab. He is a very good driver. He knows the best way to get friends through the city traffic.

People who drive their own cars to work must be sure that they have enough gas. This woman works at a gasoline station. She enjoys helping people take care of their cars.

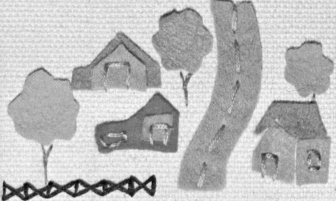

The Bay Area Rapid Transit (BART) is a very modern way to travel. BART trains are smooth and fast. They are run by a computer. But even BART knows that people on the go need friends!

Our Trip

Annie Moorecroft

PART ONE Two Washingtons

I'm Sandy Edwards.
I have a mother and a father.
I have a big brother, Jimmy.

Last Sunday we all took a trip.
We went on a trip to Washington.
It was a long car trip.

Jimmy and I were sitting
in the back of the car.
Mother was sitting with Daddy.
I had to sit next to Jimmy.
It wasn't much fun.

Jimmy knows a lot.
And he likes to show off.
"There are two Washingtons,"
Jimmy said.
"One is a city.
The other is a state.
Do you know the one we are going to?"

I didn't know anything about Washington.
But I didn't want Jimmy to know that.
So I didn't say anything to him.
I just looked out the window.

"You don't know anything, do you?"
said Jimmy.
"We are going to the city of Washington.
That's Washington, D.C.
We can't go to the state of
Washington.
It's so far from here it would
take us two days to get there."

"The state of Washington is too far
to get there in two days,"
said my father.

Washington

Washington,
D.C.

"See?" I said to Jimmy.
"You don't know so much."

"Do you know that Washington was
named for someone?" asked Jimmy.

"Everyone knows that," I said.
"It was named for George Washington.
And I know that the White House
is in Washington, too."

"Yes, but George Washington didn't
live in it," Jimmy said.

"Who said he did live in it?" I asked.
"And get out of my place.
Mother, he's got his legs
in my part of the car."

Mother said, "Now, Sandy."

"Jimmy," said my father.
"Can't you and Sandy be good
when we go on a trip?"

"Sandy," said my mother.
"Come up here with me
and get some sleep.
We won't get to our motel
for a long time."

So I did.
I was sleeping when the car
stopped at our motel.

193

PART TWO

Washington, D.C.

It was dark when we reached the motel.
It was too dark to see anything
of Washington.
So we went right to bed.

When it was light, we went out to see
the city.
We went to the White House.
It's beautiful there.

Then we stopped to look at
the cherry trees.
There were pink flowers all over them.
I wanted to pick some
of the pink flowers.
But Mother said I couldn't.
So I looked for the most beautiful
cherry tree of all.
I stood next to the pink tree.
And Daddy took my picture.

My father told us that the
Washington Monument was not too far
from the White House.
So we walked from the White House
to the Monument.
The Washington Monument goes
up and up.
And you can see all over the city
from the Monument.
Jimmy thought that was the best part
of the trip.

But the very best part for me
was at night.
We went back to the cherry trees.
My father said, "Look."
And there in the back of the trees
I saw the Washington Monument.
There were lots of lights near it.

"Isn't that beautiful!" said Mother.

She had my hand and Jimmy's hand.
I put my other hand in Daddy's hand.
And there we were, in the night,
looking at that light.
That was the very best part
of my trip to Washington.

Slow Down!

A comma says, "Slow down but don't stop."

One day after school, Jill wanted to play.
She went to see her friend, Mike.
"I just picked some berries, Jill,"
said Mike.
"Do you want to eat some berries with
my brother, Teddy, and me?"

So Mike, Jill, and Mike's brother, Teddy,
sat down to eat.
They had apples, cookies, and berries.

Punctuation Cues. Read the first sentence to the children. Exaggerate the pause as a way of illustrating the purpose of a comma. Have the children read the sentences orally. Listen for the pause in their voices at each comma.

The Camel Who Went for a Walk

Jack Tworkov

It was that quiet time in the forest.
Night was just about over.
All the forest animals were sleeping.
No one was moving.
Everything was very, very quiet.

The tiger had been sleeping
by a tree near the road.
Just then he opened his eyes.
The tiger heard something.
And he saw what it was.
It was a camel.

It was a beautiful camel with brown eyes.
The camel was out for her morning walk.
She looked as she walked.
She stopped to smell some forest flowers.
The tiger didn't take his eyes off the camel
as she came down the road.

"She will come by this tree," he thought.
"Then I will jump on her."

But the tiger was not the only one
who saw the camel walking down the road.
Up in the tree over the tiger
sat a little monkey.
The monkey saw what the tiger was going to do.

So he reached for a nut.
He said, "When the tiger jumps
on the camel, I'll throw this on his head."

The beautiful camel didn't know
what was going on in the tree.
So she walked on down the road.

But the tiger and the monkey were not
the only ones who saw the camel.
A little squirrel saw what was going on.
He climbed up in back of the monkey.
The monkey's eyes were on the camel.
He didn't see the squirrel.

I'll wait for the monkey to throw
the nut at the tiger," said the squirrel.
"Then I'll bite the monkey's tail."

The beautiful camel didn't know
what was going on in the tree.
So she walked on down the road.

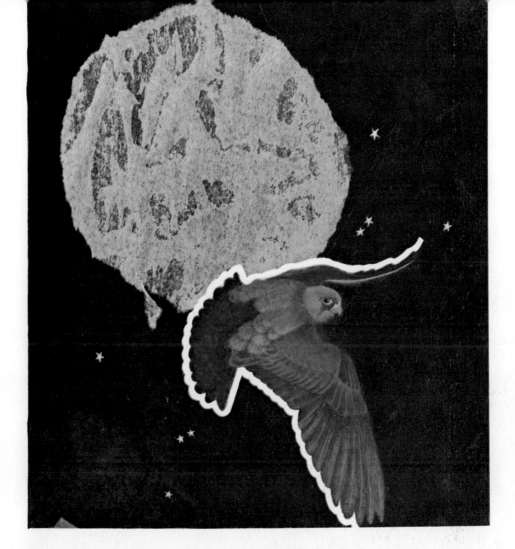

But the tiger, the monkey,
and the squirrel were not the only ones
who saw the camel.
A little bird saw what was going on.

"I know what I'll do," said the bird.
"The squirrel will bite the monkey's tail.
Then I'll fly down on the squirrel's head."

The animals waited.
Everything was quiet.
Now the camel was very near the tree.
The tiger was about to jump.
The monkey was about
to throw the nut.
The squirrel was about to bite.
And the bird was about to fly down.
But just then the camel stopped!

"It's time to go home now,"
said the camel.
"I have walked too long.
I have work to do."

And she walked back up the road.

The tiger just sat by the tree.
He looked at the camel as she walked
up the road.
He didn't jump on the camel.
And the monkey didn't throw the nut.
The squirrel didn't bite
the monkey's tail.
And the bird didn't jump
on the squirrel's head.
The animals didn't do anything.
They just sat where they were.

No one said anything.
No one made a noise.
Then the little bird began to laugh.
The squirrel heard the bird.
And he began to laugh, too.
The monkey began jumping up and down.
They made so much noise!
The other animals in the forest
couldn't sleep.

"What is going on?" asked a chipmunk.

"Not a thing," said the bird.

And he began to laugh all over again.

Camel

On the brown camel's back
    is a very big bump
And that is called
    a camel's hump.
He lives in the desert
    in a very hot land
And nibbles on palm leaves
    and sleeps on the sand.

—Nita Jonas

Margaret Wise Brown

Where Have You Been?

Little Old Cat
Little Old Cat
Where have you been?
To see this and that
Said the Little Old Cat
That's where I've been.

Little Old Squirrel
Little Old Squirrel
Where have you been?
I've been out on a whirl
Said the Little Old Squirrel
That's where I've been.

Little Old Fish
Little Old Fish
Where do you swim?
Wherever I wish
Said the Little Old Fish
That's where I swim.

Little Brown Bird
Little Brown Bird
Where do you fly?
I fly in the sky
Said the Little Brown Bird
That's where I fly.

Little Old Toad
Little Old Toad
Where have you been?
I've been way up the road
Said the Little Old Toad
That's where I've been.

Little Old Frog
Little Old Frog
Where have you been?
I've been sitting on a log
Said the Little Old Frog
That's where I've been.

Little Old Mole
Little Old Mole
Where have you been?
Down a long dark hole
Said the Little Old Mole
That's where I've been.

Little Old Bee
Little Old Bee
Where have you been?
In a pink apple tree
Said the Little Old Bee
That's where I've been.

Little Old Bunny
Little Old Bunny
Why do you run?
I run because it's fun
Said the Little Old Bunny
That's why I run.

Little Old Mouse
Little Old Mouse
Why run down the clock?
To see if the tick
Comes after the tock
I run down the clock.

Little Old Rook
Little Old Rook
Where do you look?
At the very last page
Of this very same book
Said the Little Old Rook.

New Words

14. *Kim*, Rosa
15. apartment
    her
16. *Kim's*
    Rosa's
    take
    alone
20. elevator
    buttons
    tried
    reach
21. *jump**
    button
22. *opened*
    this
    floor
27. *picked*
29. Edward
    would
    Edward's
    next
    nights
30. school
    worked
31. *sometimes*
    after
    apples**

    brothers
32. *that's, bad*
33. *wants*
35. Jimmy*
    lives
    about
39. *isn't*
    he's
    Jimmy's
41. walk
    walked
    without
    forget
44. forgot
    liking
49. *leg,* cousin
50. *asks*
    cousin's
51. fly
    thank
    telling
52. daddy-longlegs
    legs
56. crab
59. help
60. *helping*
64. red

    green
    thumb
    grew
    Mr. Greenthumb
    Mr. Greenthumb's
66. *grow*
67. *smell*
68. every, *smells*
71. *talk*
    wait
    waited
    doctor
    still
72. *waiting*
75. *try*
76. *sat*
80. paint
81. *seeds*
82. their, *thanks*
88. Maggie
    middle
    Ellen
    Mike
89. clothes
    Ellen's
    fit
    ones

own

room

90. away, *run*

91. *Maggie's*

93. *part*

   tryouts

   Mrs. Cook

95. *Mrs. Chang*

96. *noon,* stage

97. *jumps*

98. kangaroo

99. *everyone*

100. *jumping*

   called

101. *Mrs. Chang's*

   helped

   over

105. *care, being*

108. *spring*

   hats

   everywhere

   birds

   singing

109. *hat*

   Belinda

   we'll

110. head

111. *bowl*

112. mirror

another

113. aunt

   Belinda's

115. found

   Grandma

   box

116. *wear*

118. *plant, pot*

124. Lassies

   just

   wish

   how

   named

   Lassie

125. *turtle*

126. *wag*

128. tweet

129. Walter

   kittens

130. throw

   ball

   bring

134. Bert's

   berries

   Bert

   any

   other

   winter

   cold

cave

137. *eating*

   climb

   near

138. *fox*

   began

139. *why*

   because

   rabbits

158. Carmen

   somewhere

159. *Carmen's*

160. family

   took

   Pablo

   Sunday's

   Sunday

   only

   never

   anywhere

161. *wouldn't*

162 *as*

   think

   special

163. story

   please

   Pablo's

   showed

   real

164. *what's*
oh
aren't
166. *paints*
167. tiger
painted
168. *coming*
us
kangaroos
tigers
zoo
171. *Browns*
moving
putting
boxes
172. *Bobby*
gave
Ben
173. *last*
Mrs. O'Hara
174. men
climbed
Bobby's
father
175. *there's*
177. off
178. *soon*
reached
doors

rooms
smelled
179. *toys*
tonight
our
180. *bedroom*
same
treehouse
182. *Dan*
188. *trip*
Washingtons
Washington
long
sitting
knows
state
189. anything
190. *far*
days
George
192. motel
194. *dark*
light
beautiful
cherry
pink
most
stood
196. monument

best
198. lights
hand
Daddy's
202. camel
everything
203. been
eyes
heard
something
205. *walking*
nut
207. *monkey's*
bite
209. *squirrel's*
218 I've
219. whirl
220. wherever
222. *toad, way*
223. log
224. *mole, hole*
225. *bee**
apple
226. *bunny*
227. *clock*
tick
tock
229. *rook*
page

232